D0424064

The Modern Spirituality Series

Bede Griffiths

The Modern Spirituality Series

Metropolitan Anthony of Sourozh

Henri Nouwen

Lionel Blue

John Main

Thomas Merton

Carlo Carretto

Michael Ramsey

Jean Vanier

Dietrich Bonhoeffer

Bede Griffiths

Bede Griffiths

Bede Griffiths

Selections from his writings
Introduced and edited by
Peter Spink

Templegate Publishers
Springfield, Illinois

First published in 1990 by
Darton, Longman and Todd Ltd
89 Lillie Road, London SW6 1UD

First published in 1992 in the United States by
Templegate Publishers
302 East Adams St./P.O. Box 5152
Springfield, IL 62705

ISBN 0-87243-199-1

The cover photograph of Rene Magritte's
"The Tempest" is reproduced
with the permission of the Wadsworth Atheneum,
Hartford, Connecticut. Bequest of Kay Sage Tanguy.

Contents

Introduction

I first met Bede Griffiths on a bleak November day in the kitchen of a South London vicarage. It was an incongruous picture. Clad in his saffron robe this one-time Prinknash monk was inspecting the curry specially prepared by the vicar's wife for this distinguished visitor from India.

The meeting was brief. Nevertheless, in the half-hour shared together after the meal, we quickly found ourselves on common ground: India, where I too had spent some years as a missionary, and the 'perennial philosophy' which he passionately believed could be found at the heart of all the great religions.

For me this was, to say the least, a significant encounter, an affirmation of my own spiritual pilgrimage and ministry. I knew that we must meet again.

It was several years before this was to happen and this time in his monastery or Ashram in southern India. In the meantime my daughter, who had been born in India, had written the biography of this Roman Catholic monk-cum-sanyasi and I had read and heard a great deal about his life and work.

Approaching the ashram for the first time one might be forgiven for mistaking it for a Hindu temple. Here there was no imposition of signs and symbols alien to the culture of India. The carvings of the temple tower were those of familiar Christian saints, yet their appearance was almost identical to that of the innumerable gods and goddesses that adorn a typical southern Indian temple.

The central act of daily worship at the ashram is the Mass, its outward form an expression through symbols familiar to every Hindu — fire, incense, holy water and oils. Yet the eucharistic action, the offering up of all creation to the Father through the Son was crystal clear. Without doubt this remarkable man's lifelong struggle to bring about a 'marriage of East and West' had been achieved in worship. How had all this been achieved and what were the influences that had combined to give birth to this vision?

Alan Richard Griffiths, the youngest of four children, was born in December 1906 in the south of England. His father has been described as a 'middle-class failed businessman' who, having lost all his money, seems to have faded early into not very great significance in Alan's life. By his own account, described in his book *The Golden String,* Alan received little or no religious instruction from his parents, who were respectable Church of England. Perhaps surprisingly, his father was very fond of singing the hymns of the then fashionable evangelists Sankey and Moody. But beyond the ethics inherent in a conventional English and Anglican background, formal religion appears to have played little part in Alan's childhood.

An ever-probing mind wedded to a deep inner response to the mystery of creation led Alan during his adolescence at Christ's Hospital into avid and wide reading. From Thomas Hardy he gleaned an acute awareness of the rhythm of nature and a sense of the tragedy of human existence. Coupled with his study of Greek classical tragedy this deepened a growing conviction that it is through tragedy that the deepest human values are revealed.

During his last term at Christ's Hospital before going up to Magdalen College, Oxford, he had an experience so profound that he later spoke of this as one of the decisive events of his life. Walking alone in the country at sunset, his senses became acutely sharpened. The sound of birdsong came to him as he had never heard it before, a hawthorn tree, the sun setting over the playing-fields, a lark singing on the wing and the veil of dusk descending upon all, overwhelmed him with an 'awful' sense of the divine presence. That evening his consciousness had been awakened to another dimension of existence.

In the language of the nature mystic, the path of 'extrovertive mysticism' was opening up before him. Already it was becoming clear that what Hinduism describes as 'God-realization' was for him to be through an awareness of the divine reality behind the outer forms of creation. He was penetrating the mystery of the cosmos. Unconsciously at this stage he had found 'the end of Blake's Golden String'...

> I give you the end of a golden string.
> Only wind it into a ball,

It will lead you in at Heaven's gate
Built in Jerusalem's wall.

At Oxford his mind feasted on the classics. At the same time he was intuitively drawn towards Wordsworth, Shelley, Keats and Blake. Through them his awareness of the inscrutable mystery behind nature was powerfully increased.

It is clear from his autobiography, *The Golden String,* that a two-way creative relationship developed between Alan and his tutor, C. S. Lewis. By this time Lewis had passed through atheism and had reached the stage of belief in a universal Spirit, though he would not yet call this Spirit God. It was a conception which appealed strongly to Alan and one which was for ever afterwards at the heart of his understanding of ultimate reality.

Conscious and personal faith in Christ was to come much later when he disciplined himself to 'search the Scriptures' in a systematic way. The day was soon to come when the Epistles of St Paul with their insistence upon God's love for us, God's gift of love, were to speak directly to his heart, so bringing him to Christian faith and giving him a rationale for his inner journey. This step-by-step probing and praying, coupled with an underlying search for order in all things led him almost inexorably into the Roman Catholic Church and soon after into ordination and the life of the Benedictines. There through their monastic disciplines he became Father Bede. In 1955 began his momentous ministry in southern India.

Many of the visitors to my own community in England had visited the Saccidananda ashram, and during visits to Australia and New Zealand I found myself again and again asked the questions: 'Do you know Bede Griffiths?' and 'What do you think of his books?' The questioners came from a great variety of backgrounds: practicing Catholics; many who had left the Church and were seeking a way back which they could take with integrity; 'New Age' seekers and agnostics of every variety.

Clearly the ashram was not only a place of pilgrimage, particularly for the young of many countries, but a place where people representing great diversity of beliefs were experiencing an essential unity in Christ. It was this which so strongly attracted me and clearly this was the magnetic pull which today draws thousands to this powerhouse of meditation and prayer in a remote part of southern India.

The whole atmosphere of the ashram, as in every place where prayer is the central activity, is that of 'creative stillness' where not even what in the West is called 'spiritual reading' is allowed to intrude. For although the ashram has an extensive library, in the center set apart for meditation is a notice: 'Reading is not permitted here'.

For over thirty years Bede Griffiths has labored to communicate his understanding of the marriage of East and West which he has likened to the bringing together of the faculties of reason and intuition, the active and the passive, the male and the female. This is at the heart both of his spirituality and of his interpretation of Christianity through the myths and symbols of Hinduism.

What is this spirituality which has such a universal appeal today? It is perhaps important to begin with what it is not. Quite clearly it is not syncretistic, that is, an attempt to intermesh Christianity and Hinduism into one amorphous and in some way 'super' religion.

Never does Father Bede pretend that at the level of doctrine and belief there are not very great differences between Hinduism and Christianity. Indeed, he believes fervently in the necessity of the growth of understanding between the religions, and has himself spent much time and energy in advancing the cause of interfaith dialogue. Yet he is equally clear that this is not the level at which real unity is to be discovered. And here the word 'discovered' is important for Bede's understanding. For the unity which has preoccupied his thinking and energized his ministry is that unity which the mystics of all religions have always known and shared. It is the unity of the opened heart.

What comes through with great clarity from all his writings is that diversity and division exist and will always exist at the level of beliefs but that experientially, in the knowledge of the heart, we find a profound sharing in the mystery of godliness.

His perspectives are those of a new ecumenism where the discovery of oneness is the same in kind as that discovered by 'divided'

Christians when less than half a century ago they began to pray together.

Bede has no doubt that this unity is 'Christ-centred' and it is here that his understanding of the Cosmic Christ is so important. There is certainly nothing 'heretical' nor even novel about this. It is thoroughly Pauline and biblical. Writing to the Christians at Corinth, St Paul refers to the supernatural food and drink which the Israelites found in the wilderness.

This food and drink he declared 'was Christ' (1 Corinthians 10). So whilst Bede sees Christ as perfectly revealed in Jesus and takes no issue with orthodox definitions of Christology, he is equally insistent that this same Christ is active at every stage of history and in the hearts of human beings, regardless of religious boundaries. The authentic signs of Christ's presence are the fruits of the Spirit. This is the Christ who, as the 'Alpha and Omega' of the Christian revelation, embraces all time and space and gives meaning and purpose to all creation.

It is this recognition of the Christ who 'fills all things' which gives Bede such a powerful rapport with many young people who have clearly entered into a valid experience of the grace of God outside of the structures of the Christian Church in our day.

In this sense Bede's spirituality is very much a contemporary spirituality. For whilst it can be articulated and expressed without reservation in terms of the Christian faith it gives sympathetic expression to what has been described as the 'new consciousness' in religion.

What is this new consciousness? Today there is much evidence in the Western world of a new awakening to that which Hinduism has always emphasized: the divine immanence or indwelling. In Christian terms this may be seen as a consciousness of the indwelling Christ, so central to the Pauline Epistles yet so absent in any developed form of traditional Christian spirituality in the West.

The spirituality which emerges clearly through Bede's writings hinges all the time on this indwelling of the Divine. Yet this is not an isolated nor individual God-consciousness. Bede sees it not only in relationship to the human being but in all creation. Yet this is much more than the current ecological concern which, clothed in a religious dress, is often incorrectly described as creation spirituality. For Bede creation is never an end in itself. All creation is shot through with consciousness. Furthermore this consciousness which is always evolving finds its apex in the human being. Here he relates closely to the Indian philosopher Sri Aurobindo and to the Jesuit priest-scientist Teilhard de Chardin.

For Bede 'the Body of Christ' can never be confined to the visible Church, still less to one ecclesiastical tradition. Neither can it be thought of as excluding all creation. 'Every religion,' he declares, 'has contributed to its growth.' It is constituted of all those who, in the language of Hinduism, have in some measure 'realized the Self' within the depths of their being.

In this bringing together of the Hindu experience of God's immanence and the revealed Christian 'mystery' of the Christ within, who, declares St Paul, is our 'hope of glory,' Bede sees both as relating to the true Self. This is the one Self which may be described as the Cosmic Being or Man. Its final manifestation is the parousia or 'second coming' of Christ.

Like many pioneers and prophets before him Bede has suffered misunderstandings and calumny from those elements within the Church who have felt fearful and threatened by his insistence upon a Christ who 'fills all things.' His ministry has the hallmark of one who at whatever cost has followed the path which the Spirit, the Holy Spirit, has opened before him. For him it may be said 'there are no boundaries, only horizons.'

In this breadth of vision and comprehension Bede is aware of great movements of convergence. Science, mysticism, the holistic movement within Western medicine and the awakening concern for the future of the planet: all these constitute essential elements of his spiritual perceptions. He frequently refers to 'a new vision of reality' which is now manifesting itself in Western physics, where the mechanistic view of creation as perceived by Newton is giving way to a creation seen as one organic whole, and where increasingly it is recognized that the scientist himself as the observer must be taken into account if we are to understand the nature of what is being observed. So the mystical awareness that 'the observed and the observer are one' is now finding an affirmation (albeit reluctant) from within the scientific disciplines.

Yet with all this breadth of vision and depth of insight Bede is ever a faithful son of the Roman Catholic Church into which he was received over fifty years ago. The Benedictine monastic tradition operates deep within his psyche and it is from the foundation of a thorough training in philosophy and theology that his ever-probing and speculative mind continues to inquire.

Undoubtedly it is this combination of deep roots and openness of mind and heart, which at eighty-three gives Father Bede Griffiths such a strong appeal to the young who still pour into his ashram from the Western world. Yet in spite of his own deep appreciation of and indebtedness to Hindu philosophy and spirituality, he is quite clear that the way forward for those 'searchers after God' is to return to the West and there in the context of their own history and culture to work out and apply the deep insights they have gained into the nature of truth.

Father Bede has no time for those uncritical imitations of Hinduism, the adopting of forms and rituals which so characterized much of the pseudo-spirituality of the young in the 1960s and 1970s. His is no easy spirituality. For him God-consciousness, self-realization, a Christ-centered life are the fruits of disciplines continuously practiced. Yet these disciplines must never be the imposition of an asceticism which smothers and represses those emotional and psychic elements which are all part of a fully developed human being.

Human beings are tripartite, that is, body, soul, and spirit. No philosophy of life which fails to take all these dimensions into account is adequate for human beings, whether Eastern or Western, if they are to evolve to their full potential at the end of the twentieth century.

The dynamic which has operated so manifestly through his dedication to the marriage of East and West is undiminished, for it relates powerfully to the questions which are being posed so widely today.

Father Bede stands at a point of intersection between the old and the new, between East and West, between the deposit of faith as received by the Roman Catholic Church and the essential unity of all mystics. His message transcends all boundaries of culture and religion. It is that of 'knowing Christ and the power of his resurrection.'

PETER SPINK

East and West

Humanity is divided because man is divided in himself. The two great traditions of East and West stand as the two sides of understanding of man. So far these two traditions have grown independently with little relation beyond occasional rivalry. The time has come to integrate them.

In the West today the masculine aspect, the rational, the aggressive power of the mind is dominant, while in the East the feminine aspect, the intuitive aspect of the mind prevails.

The future of the world depends on the 'marriage' of these two minds, the conscious and the unconscious, the rational and the intuitive, the active and the passive. This 'marriage' must take place first within the individual. Then only can external union take place.

Experience of God

The body experiences the physical world, the soul (psyche) the psychological, the spirit alone has the capacity to contemplate God.

It is here that God's spirit acts within the human being and where we become aware of our identity as children of God.

This is beautifully expressed by St Paul when he tells us that the Spirit of God bears witness with our spirit that we are children of God (Romans 8:16).

The Spirit is present in every human being. It may be totally concealed but it is always there and without it we cannot be fully human.

As the spirit learns to contemplate God, the categories of the rational mind—subject and object, mind and matter, time and space—necessary as they are for completeness of being, are transcended. When we consciously uncover this dimension of our full humanity we become fully integrated human beings. Body, soul and spirit are in communion with God.

Man and creation

The physical universe is a web of interdependent relationships. There is nothing in the world that is not dependent in some way upon everything else. This is affirmed by modern science.

The smallest movement on earth has its repercussions throughout the universe. Within this interrelated order human beings have a special potential and power.

Through meditation we dicover and uncover our links with the whole creation. We put ourselves into harmony with the universe and integrate ourselves with all humanity.

Redeemed mankind then strives towards creation's ultimate destiny. As St Paul puts it in Romans 8:22-23, 'The whole creation groans in travail, waiting for the redemption of the children of God.'

This is a conscious offering up of creation to the Creator. Herein lies the uniqueness of the human being.

A redemptive sacrifice

Jesus was a man in whom body and soul were pure instruments of the indwelling spirit. In him human destiny has been fulfilled.

Whereas in the universe as we know it there is conflict at every level, and body and soul are in conflict with one another, in Jesus this conflict has been overcome. Body and soul have been restored in unity with the spirit, and a power of unification has been released into the world.

So we are able to see the death of Jesus and the free surrender of his life on the cross to the Father as a cosmic event.

Certain events, that is, the emergence of life on this planet, the awakening of consciousness in man, mark critical changes in the evolution of the world. The death of Jesus was an event of this kind. It marked the point of transition of the human consciousness to the Divine, the point where the human being was totally surrendered, body and soul, to the divine Being. In this sense the death of Jesus can be called 'a redemptive sacrifice'; it is an offering of human nature to the divine which 'redeems,' that is, restores human nature to its unity with the divine nature.

Service and detachment

Acceptable service done for God is that which proceeds from non-attachment. To be detached from oneself, from people, from things and to act with a completely pure motivation is difficult but that is the only true service for God and for humanity.

According to the Gospels, we have to be totally detached even from father and mother and wife and children and lands and all that we have. Then we love totally and serve perfectly.

It is equally wrong to be either averted from or attached to somebody or something. When we are totally detached then we are able to see clearly and deal with the situation without reaction, with a calm and peaceful mind and with a true understanding.

The yoga of love

Yoga means the practice of a spiritual discipline. Bhatki yoga is the discipline of love, that is, to open our hearts to love.

Love in its fullness is both the love of God for us and our love for God. In the *Bhagavad Gita* we read: 'Hear again my Word supreme, the deepest secret of silence. Because I love thee well I will speak to thee words of salvation' (chapter 18).

This is the nature of the religious experience. To know the love of God is to reflect on it, to realize it, to experience it in the heart. This love, as St Paul says, 'passes knowledge,' and is poured into the heart by the Holy Spirit who is given us.

By entering into his heart man discovers not only that he can love God but that he is loved by God.

Intuitive wisdom

Intuition is knowledge which derives not from observation and experience or from concepts and reason, but from the mind's reflection on itself.

What distinguishes the human mind above all else is not its powers of observation and experiment which animals also possess in some degree, not its powers of logical deduction, but its power of self-reflection. For the human mind is so structured that it is always present to itself.

Intuition may be described as the passive intellect. It may be likened to a still, clear pool of reflection. It cannot be produced but the condition which permits the intuition to function is that of the mind 'stayed upon God'.

Wordsworth describes the process in 'Lines composed a few miles above Titern Abbey':

> Felt in the blood, and felt along the heart,
> And passing even into the purer mind
> with tranquil restoration.

Only when we offer our minds to God do we receive the illumination of his wisdom.

God our Mother and Father

God is both Mother and Father. The Oriental tradition has always recognized this.

The biblical name for the spirit *(ruah)* is feminine and in the later Syriac tradition which preserved the same name the Holy Spirit was spoken of as Mother. In the Old Testament there is the tradition of feminine wisdom.

It is possible to see in the Holy Spirit the feminine aspect of God in the Trinity. The source of the Trinity is both Father and Mother. The Son or Word is the source of order in the universe. The Holy Spirit is the feminine principle of receptivity, an infinite capacity for love which receives perpetually the outflowing of love through the Son and returns it to its source in the Father. In Christ, this perfect unity of male and female, this yin and yang, are brought together, for 'in Christ there is neither male nor female...'

Unity and separateness

The human person is a center of consciousness which is capable of infinite extension. As it grows it becomes more and more integrated with the whole complex of persons who make up humanity.

We become more ourselves as we enter more deeply into relationship with others. We do not lose ourselves but we lose our sense of separation and division.

This is essentially a mystery of love. When two people love one another they do not lose their distinction of person, they become more fully personal.

The whole process of evolution, as Teilhard de Chardin saw it, is a process of personalization. The ultimate goal of humanity is a communion of persons in love.

This is what was revealed in St John's Gospel when Jesus prayed for his disciples 'that they may be one as you, Father, are in me and I in you, that they may be one in us' (John 17:21).

The Cosmic Christ

In Jesus we see mirrored and perfectly revealed the Cosmic Being, the principle of the Godhead active in all history.

The Cosmic Christ may be seen working in and through the Israelites and speaking through the patriarchs and prophets. In like manner the same Cosmic Being may be seen moving in and through all the great religions in every age.

With the great intermingling of the cultures of East and West witnessed during this century, it has become increasingly difficult not to recognize this activity of the universal Christ. For it has become increasingly apparent that nowhere in the world and at no period of history has God left himself without a witness.

Christ is indeed the Alpha and the Omega, the first and the last, the one who embraces all history in meaning and purpose.

Christ's mystical Body

From the beginning of history the Body of Christ, which is the Body of a true humanity, has been growing age by age and every religion has contributed to its growth.

There is one self who has become incarnate in humanity. Humanity in the total course of history is the body of this self.

What becomes of the individual self in this knowledge of the one self? Without doubt the individual loses all sense of separation from the one and enters into the experience of total unity, but the individual still exists. As in nature every element is a unique reflection of the one reality, so every human being is a unique center of consciousness in the universal consciousness.

Every person grows as he opens himelf to the totality of personal being which is found in the supreme person.

This is what is expressed in the doctrine of the mystical Body of Christ. This Body embraces all humanity in the unity of the one person of Christ. This is described by St Augustine as follows: 'There is only one Christ loving himself.'

Mindfulness

The great spiritual teachers of all religions have themselves practiced and taught mindfulness.

To be mindful is to live in the present moment, not to be imprisoned in the past nor anticipating a future that may never happen.

When we are fully aware of the present, life is transformed and strain and stress disappear.

So much of modern life is a feverish anticipation of future activity and excitement. We have to learn to step back from this into the freedom and possibility of the present.

The ancient wisdom

Western science is slowly beginning to rediscover the ancient tradition of wisdom, according to which mind and matter are interdependent and complementary aspects of one reality. This same process can also be observed in Western medicine where there is a gradual recognition that all disease is psychosomatic and that the human body cannot be properly treated apart from the soul.

A knowledge is slowly being recovered which was universal in the ancient world that there is no such thing as matter apart from mind or consciousness.

Consciousness is latent in every particle of matter and the mathematical order which science discovers in the universe is due to the working of this universal consciousness within it.

In human nature latent consciousness begins to come into actual consciousness, and as human consciousness evolves it grows more and more conscious of the universal consciousness in which it is grounded — God the very ground of our being.

Consciousness and matter

Modern physics is changing our view of the whole structure of the universe. Matter is no longer conceived of as an extended substance in society, extending beyond ourselves. Matter is now perceived as a 'web of interdependent relations' forming an organic whole.

Science is also telling us that the physical world cannot be separated from the psyche, from the consciousness. Instead of a separate extended world and a separate mind, we have a field of energy which is also interdependent with the whole psychological world, the world of consciousness.

The world can no longer be separate from consciousness; so do we see the significance of St Paul's vision of all nature as in travail and waiting for the manifestation of the children of God (Romans 8).

The true Church

Wherever man wakes to consciousness and knowing himself in his basic intuitive consciousness as open to the transcendent mystery of existence, the power of the Spirit in him is drawing him to eternal life.

The Church is man become conscious of his destiny as a son of God. In the biblical perspective Adam is man created in the image and likeness of God and called to be a son of God.

When Adam sins he fails to respond to the spirit and falls back on his limited time-bound nature. The upward evolution from matter through life and consciousness to eternal life in the spirit is checked, but at the same time the mystery of redemption begins. A new power of the spirit enters creation and begins to draw man back into the life of the spirit.

In this sense the Church is present in humanity from the beginning of history.

Meditation

Meditation has been described as the direct path to God. Until recent years Western thought has largely regarded the practice of meditation as Eastern, even as non-Christian.

As a result of the influence of Eastern culture on the Western world and the current interest in Indian religion and philosophy many in the West now follow the meditative path.

Meditation consists in learning to focus and to control the mind. When the mind is stilled, then the light of the intellect begins to shine. The mind is ordinarily scattered and dissipated, but gather the mind into one and then the pure light shines in the mirror which is oneself.

Speech is the movement by which we go out of ourselves to communicate to another. Meditation takes us within ourselves. It is a process of inner withdrawal, a centering in the place of inner detachment, a staying of the mind upon God.

God within and beyond

There are two different ways of looking at God. You can think of him as above and you can pray to him and ask his grace to descend. You can kneel in penitence and ask for mercy.

Equally you can think of God as immanent, present in the earth, in the water, in the air.

These two different ways are complementary. Just as a Christian starting from above discovers the Holy Spirit as immanent and realizes the presence of God in the whole creation around him, so the Hindu starting with the immanence of God in creation, in the human heart, rises to the idea of God beyond the creation and beyond humanity.

These are two complementary visions and we have to bring them together in our lives so that each enriches the other.

Beyond religion

It is no longer possible today for one religion to live in isolation from other religions. In almost every country people of different religions are meeting with one another and being compelled to face their differences.

More and more the necessity for contact is being realized. Those who attempt to do so are feeling that dialogue when properly understood is not a compromise but a process of enrichment by which each religion opens itself to the truth to be found in the other religion, and the two parties grow together in a common desire for truth.

Each religion has to hold to its own tradition, yet to allow that tradition to grow as it opens itself to other aspects of truth. So we realize that truth is one, but that it has many faces and each religion is an aspect of that face. The one truth is perceived to be manifesting itself under different signs and symbols.

Discernment

Discernment is to see beyond the veils imposed by the senses; to see things as they are.

Such capacity to see comes to those who operate from the deep center within themselves. It implies detachment and freedom; detachment from impressions received from the world of the senses and freedom from personal desire.

In India discernment or discrimination has always been central to an understanding of what constitutes spirituality, for to follow the spiritual path involves withdrawal from the 'unreal to the real.' So does the heart become open to divine wisdom.

Unknowing

As we grow into Christian maturity we may find
ourselves drawn beyond all images and concepts
of God into what has been called 'the cloud of
unknowing.' Here we find ourselves at the
center of a paradox, for intellectually we do not
know, yet ultimately we know that which cannot be grasped by the intellect.

This has been the experience of all the mystics.
Today the 'unknowing' is entered into by many
who, divided by concepts, images and symbols,
nevertheless are feeling a unity in God.

Beyond all knowledge

The ultimate mystery cannot be named, cannot be properly conceived.

This is the foundation of all theology, this understanding that the ultimate mystery of being, by whatever name it is known, cannot be properly named or conceived. All words which are used about this mystery are signs or symbols of the ineffable and are of value only in so far as they point towards this mystery and enable its presence to be experienced in the 'heart' or the inner 'center' of the person beyond speech and thought.

This presence cannot be known by the senses or by the rational mind. It is unseen but seeing; unheard but hearing; unperceived but perceiving; unknown but knowing.

The Church and truth

What is the essential truth signified by the organization, doctrine and rituals of the Church?

It is the presence of the divine life among men, the mystery of being which is the ground of all religion and of all existence manifesting itself in the presence of Jesus Christ.

In this revelation the mystery of being reveals itself as a mystery of love, of an eternal love ever rising from the depths of being in the Godhead and manifesting itself in the total self-giving of Jesus on the cross.

The Church has no other purpose than to communicate this love, to create a community of love, to unite all men in the eternal ground of being which is present in the heart of every man.

A communion of love

In the ultimate reality there is revealed not merely an identity but a communion. The Christian revelation is that the Godhead itself, the ultimate reality, is a commitment of persons, a communion of powers in love. This gives a further dimension to our understanding of reality.

There cannot be love without two. In the Christian concept the Godhead itself is love, a communion of love. There is a distinction within the Godhead itself, a distinction beyond our comprehension which we endeavor to express theologically in terms of persons and relations. These are human terms pointing to the reality. The reality is that God is love, that there is something with corresponds to personal communion in love in the Godhead and we are called to share in that communion of love.

In the mystical Body of Christ which embraces all redeemed humanity, we do not disappear in the Godhead but we discover a personal relationship of love. Each person is fulfilled and is open to the other person; it is an intercommunion of love in which each embraces the other and all are embraced in God.

A Cosmic Covenant

Before God revealed himself in a special revelation to the Jews, to Moses, to David and to the prophets, he revealed himself to Noah, and in the Hebrew understanding Noah was the Father of mankind. Mankind had been destroyed in the flood; a new mankind, foretelling the new creation, came into being and Noah was the Father of this new mankind. His three sons represented all the nations of the world known to Israel.

Noah is the Father of mankind and God made a covenant through Noah with all mankind. This covenant with Noah is the new expression of the Cosmic Covenant.

No one is outside the covenant with God. Today Christians are beginning to recognize the place of other religions within the plan of God and to realize that all are included within this Cosmic Covenant.

The Cosmic Covenant enlarges our vision, for we begin to realize that this great cosmic order should be manifested in the Church. In the cosmic sacrifice of the Mass all creation is offered in and through Christ to the Father.

Peace

Peace can only be manifested in society when there is peace within the human heart. The cause of peace is sometimes pursued with aggressiveness. This is the case when peace is no more than a concept or an ideal.

Peace communicates itself wordlessly. In India the great example of the power of peace was seen in Mahatma Gandhi whose inner peace influenced the whole nation.

Work for peace must first of all be a work within ourselves.

The union of opposites

Man and woman are equal and opposite. A women does not become more equal to man by seeking to become like a man, but by revealing his opposite character. Yet it must be recognized that every man and woman is both male and female; reason and intuition exist alike in every human being, but in the man reason is dominant whilst intuition is prominent in the woman.

In a perfect man or woman the marriage of these opposites takes place. Reason without intuition is intelligent but sterile; intuition without reason is fertile but blind.

The woman who seduces man is the blind instinct which listens to the voice of the serpent, the animal intelligence or sexuality. The feminine mind, instead of being guided by reason so as to open itself to the spirit, thus achieving the marriage of reason and intuition, surrenders to animal instinct.

The union of the male (reason) and female (intuition) gives birth to communion in the spirit and integration of the personality. Thus the serpent energy becomes the savior, as stated in St John's Gospel: 'As Moses lifted up the serpent in the wilderness, so must the Son of man be lifted up, that whoever believes in him may have eternal life' (John 3:14-15).

The transformation of all things

If the soul is transformed by participation in the divine nature so also must the body be and with the body the whole material universe.

God in Christ becomes what we are in order that we might become his 'body.'

This transformation of man by the divine life begins even now on earth, but it is only completed when man's body is also transformed by the resurrection.

When the resurrection takes place, then the whole universe is transformed together with the body of man. In this sense the whole universe becomes the 'Body of Christ.'

Man and nature will then become wholly penetrated by the divine consciousness and share alike in the bliss of the divine love which is poured out on the whole creation. Then we can say that the whole universe of insentient and sentient beings will become the 'Body of God.'

Contemplation

Contemplation is to see and to hear from the heart. It takes us beyond sense perception. It is to relate to things as they are.

All so-called spiritual knowledge is useless if simply retained in the head. It is a waste of time and leads to self-delusion. It is to know about rather than to know.

The same is true of theological knowledge. This has to be diverted towards the contemplative experience through meditation, otherwise it remains apart from life and is of no ultimate value.

Contemplative seeing is not selective. It is not processed by the brain nor conditioned by previously held concepts and attitudes. It constitutes a whole way of life, a way to be followed by the true disciple of Jesus.

Traditionally, contemplation has been thought of as an Eastern approach to religion. Action in this world has been seen as its opposite and typical of the Western understanding. Today's world requires a marriage of the two, that is, contemplation in action.

Contemplation in action

Contemplation unites us with God at a vertical level where we transcend ourselves, the world and all our problems, and experience oneness with God. It is at the same time a mode of action at the horizontal level by which we go out from the center of peace in God to the whole world. The further we go vertically towards God the further we can go horizontally towards men.

Jesus is the man who is totally given to God, to the Father, the one who is totally surrendered to the vertical movement, so that the Son always sees what the Father is doing. At the same time he was totally open to all people and to life as a whole. That is the dual movement, vertical and horizontal, of contemplation in action, action in contemplation.

This is a universal call not only for monks or for nuns or for unmarried people but for everybody who seeks God.

The universe within

There is a space within the heart in which all space is contained. Both heaven and earth are contained within it. Fire, air, sun and moon, lightning and stars—everything exists within.

When we pass beyond the mind with its measuring faculties, with its categories of time and space, we find the very ground of the universe. There all things are not dead matter as Western science has told us for so long. They are life and intelligence.

Western man has been turning outwards to the world of senses for centuries and losing himself in outer space. The time has now come to turn inwards, to learn to explore the inner space within the heart, and to make that long and exciting journey to the Center. Compared with this the exploration of the moon and planets is the play of children.

Be still

Inner stillness is necessary if we are to be in perfect control of our faculties and if we are to hear the voice of the Spirit speaking to us.

There can be no stillness without discipline, and the discipline of external silence can help us towards that inner tranquillity which is at the heart of authentic religious experience.

In meditation we take steps to achieve this stillness. We quieten our bodies and our emotions, then gradually allow the mind to become single-pointed.

Stillness within one individual can affect society beyond measure.

Symbols of God

All religions seek to demonstrate the reality of God through symbols. These symbols are seen as pointers to a transcendent reality beyond themselves.

Symbols are necessary for they make the reality present to us. Every word we use is a symbol. God is a symbol. Allah is a symbol. Yahweh is a symbol. Christ is a symbol. These are symbols we use to point to something which cannot be described or expressed.

The use of symbols points to the mystery of human life, that is, that we are pushed beyond ourselves, beyond our limits.

Symbols are powerful signposts towards reality, signs which make reality present to us but which can never exhaust and manifest reality in all its fullness.

Each religion has its sacred and revered symbols. A contemplative awareness will take us beyond all these to the one reality with which we seek unity.

A universal revelation

The Holy Spirit is at work in all creation and within all humanity, drawing all men and all things to unity in Christ, that is, into his mystical Body.

The realization of this unity begins within ourselves. From the depths of our being we learn with Christ to say 'Abba, Father.' It is there that we touch the source from which all life flows.

At the surface level of the various religions there are great diversity, differences and contradictions. As we touch one another at the deep level so we find ourselves moving from separation to unity, from contradiction to oneness and from diversity to convergence.

In every human being the Holy Spirit is present and at work. Even when ignored or denied the Spirit is moving, and drawing towards unity in Christ. He is drawing all things back to the source until we enter that absolute unity beyond all duality and are one with the Father.

Beyond phenomena

Christians have constantly to remind themselves that one cannot stop with any name for God, however holy the name may be. The name points to the person and the person points to the inexpressible mystery, the source.

When we look around at the world about us we see the earth, the sky, the water, the plants and trees, the animals and people. But what we have to do is to look behind all these phenomena and discover their hidden source. Most people stop with the phenomena; they appreciate the earth or sky or flowers or the sun or stars, they admire the beauty, but they do not try to find the hidden source of the sky and flowers, of every single thing. We see beyond only when we look with the eyes of the heart.

The second coming

Jesus left the disciples with the promise that he would return, and that this returning would constitute 'the end of the world.'

We now live at a time when there are forces present in the world capable of destroying all life on the planet and the planet itself.

We cannot know whether society will experience 'a change of heart' sufficient to avoid such destruction. We need to remind ourselves that our destiny is not in this world as it is. We have to be prepared to go beyond death. We have to die to this world and everything in it, to find the reality which does not change or pass.

When Christ appears 'in glory' it will not be in any manner we can now conceive, as we ourselves must die to ourselves in order to become part of the 'new creation.'

Then we shall enter into the fullness of truth, of wisdom and of knowledge and of love.

The true ecumenism

Christianity came out of the Semitic world of Jewish culture. Its teaching, definitions and thought were largely formed by Greek culture and philosophy. For nearly two thousand years the movement of the Church has been westwards.

The twentieth century has witnessed a powerful convergence of Western and Eastern cultures and this is profoundly affecting today's Church. Meditation, once thought to be the prerogative of Eastern and non-Christian religions, has thus opened the door into a Christ-centred spirituality for thousands of Westerners.

The immanent or indwelling God always central to Eastern spirituality is now by many seen to be at one with the Pauline doctrine of 'Christ in you, the hope of glory' (Ephesians 3).

God is one. Knowledge of the one God comes to all human beings through the opening of the heart. This is the true ecumenism. It is the true interior religion of Christ for which today there is a great yearning.

The ground of our being

The Spirit is the source, the ground of all being.
Everything comes from the Spirit and reflects its
power and light.

The energy of matter, the life in plants and
animals, the soul in man are all reflections, ef-
fects of the power and life and knowledge of the
one Spirit.

To recognize the dependence of all creatures on
the inner light and power of the Spirit is to par-
take of the Spirit's own wisdom and immortali-
ty. To refuse to recognize this dependence, to
seek to be autonomous and to control the world
is to take the path of death.

The purpose of creation was that man should
become like God, sharing in his wisdom and im-
mortality, but this can come only as we surrender all the powers of our being, of body and
soul to the power of the Spirit within.

The true self

Fully realized human beings are more than body and soul (psyche). They are body, soul and spirit. This spirit is there within every human being.

To relate consciously to the 'spirit' is, in the words of Jesus, to find the true self.

Without this 'self-realization' we live as isolated human beings. We are unfulfilled and falling short of our destiny as human beings.

United to our true or transcendental selves we find our union with Christ.

Beyond this we find a true unity or communion with others. All barriers of separation are transcended. Further still, we find a unity with all creation. The unity of mankind can never be attained on the level of body and soul alone. Only when we awaken to the true self can we find that true harmony with others and with the created order.

Harmony with the cosmos

History itself, the evolution of humanity and the world, is all part of a divine drama. The whole universe is to be taken up into the divine along with the whole of humanity in all the stages of its history. When we begin consciously to relate to this we become aware of ourselves as parts of that whole, but also the whole is present in each one of us.

Each one is a microcosm, and the macrocosm is present in each one. This is an absolute unity yet it embraces the diversity and all the multiplicity of the universe.

This affects our practical lives. If we think that the universe is ultimately unreal and that our own lives are unreal, we will live accordingly. But it will make all the difference to how we live when we realize that this universe is created by God, that it has infinite eternal value in the sight of God, and that we all form a unity which yet embraces all divinity.

So we are fulfilled in that Absolute, in our own individual being and in the whole cosmic order.

Renunciation

For anyone who is on a spiritual path, that is, the path to God, there must be an element of renunciation in this life.

In India renunciation is seen as an essential part of the spiritual growth and awakening. A man may leave his family at a certain stage of his life and go into the forest, there to find God within his soul. He gives up the comforts of life for a greater good. We do not need to follow this practice literally in order to find our 'true selves,' but we must be prepared to sacrifice legitimate things in order that we may find the space in which the spiritual life can blossom.

This is the way of the cross which leads to a kind of death and resurrection.

The sacrament of creation

The cosmic revelation is based on the belief that God reveals himself both in the human soul and in all creation.

The visible world therefore becomes an outward and visible sign of a greater reality.

This mystery is beyond thought. It is an inexpressible mystery manifesting itself in the cosmos, infinitely transcendent and not to be uttered. Indian philosophy describes it as 'not this, not this.'

Yet we ourselves are part of this creation and when we enter into the depths of our own spirit we discover this depth of God, the Lord dwelling within us. Here we encounter the cosmic person who dwells in the heart of every human being, yet embraces the whole creation and is beyond all humanity. He is the 'superior person' beyond and above all.

Resurrection

At the resurrection Jesus becomes the 'head' of
the cosmic whole, and the whole creation
becomes his Body. This Body of creation
redeemed from the forces of sin and division is
what constitutes the Church. 'He has put all
things under his feet,' says St Paul (1 Corinthians
15:27), 'and made him the head over all things
for the Church, which is his body, the fullness of
him who fills all in all.'

The Church is the fullness, the consummation of
all things, the term of the whole evolutionary
process. The Divine has taken possesssion of
nature and filled men with his presence. In other
words nature has been wholly penetrated with
consciousness, and man and nature have
become one with the eternal Spirit.

What was accomplished in Jesus through his
sacrificial death and his rebirth to eternal life is
what is destined to happen in all men and in all
creation.

Each of us is called to pass beyond sin and suffering into the new life of the resurrection.

To lose and find the self

A great many people think their body is themselves. Others think the personality is themselves. 'This personality is me, this is my self,' and so they are satisfied.

Others reflect that this personality of mine — my thoughts, feelings, desires is going to pass away when my body decays. This is not the self I am seeking, for it also belongs to the changing world.

The basic orientation of the Upanishads is found in the search for the inner self, the self beyond the body and the mind.

This is a hidden mystery. We look into the depths of our being and find this hidden mystery. In Christian terms you have discovered yourself in God. In the words of St Paul in Ephesians 3, 'The mystery long hidden is revealed, it is Christ in you, the hope of glory.'

God-realization

The Indian mind has never been content to know 'about God'; it has always sought to know God. And here there is no separation between subject and object.

To 'realize' God is to experience his presence, not in the imagination or in the intellect but in the ground of the soul from which all human faculties spring.

This is the knowledge which the Upanishads were intended to impart, the knowledge of the Self, the Knower, which is the subject not the object of thought, the ground alike of being and of thought.

To realize God in this way is to discover one's true self.

God all and in all

The world which is studied by science, the world of politics and economics, the world of social and cultural life, which most people take for reality, is a world of appearances with no ultimate reality. It is all passing away at every moment and everybody is passing with it.

The Church also belongs to this world of 'signs.' The doctrines and sacraments of the Church are human expressions or signs of the divine reality, which are likewise destined to pass away.

Christ also is the 'sacrament' of God. He is the sign of God's grace and salvation, of God's presence among men. This sign will also pass when the reality, the thing signified, is revealed. For as St Paul describes it, 'Then shall the Son himself be subject to God, that God may be all and in all' (1 Corinthians 15:28).

The Christ of history

For a Christian, Jesus is the supreme symbol or sacrament of God in man, the ultimate sign of the meaning of human existence, not a mythological figure but a unique historical person.

In Israel a conception of progressive time, of movement towards an end was developed, and Jesus enters this historical time as the one who is to bring it to its fulfillment. 'It was his purpose in the fullness of time to bring all things to a head in him' (Ephesians 1:10).

Jesus is the unique historical person whose death and resurrection mark the culmination of the history of a particular people, but at the same time he is in his actual historical existence the symbol of the ultimate meaning and purpose of human existence.

Jesus does not annul the significance of the Hindu gods. They remain of permanent significance, giving a unique insight into reality. A Christian does not therefore need to reject them but to relate them at their own proper level to the revelation of God in Christ.

Fulfillment

It is of the very nature of human love that it cannot be completely satisfied with physical contact or emotional sympathy. It seeks a radical fulfillment in total self-giving.

For some, sexual union is the way to total self-giving and self-discovery. Others may awaken to the ecstasy of love in the presence of nature, like Wordsworth; others may find it in loving service and self-sacrifice.

It is no accident that the mystical experience is sometimes described in terms of sexual union. This is not a 'sublimation' in the Freudian sense. Rather it is an opening of human nature to the full dimension of its being.

Whichever way we are destined to take leads to the discovery of the depths of the self, no longer in isolation but in the communion of love for which it was created.

The vision of god

To share in the vision of God means that we have to pass beyond all concepts of the rational mind and all images derived from the senses. We must pass into the world of non-duality, in which our present mode of consciousness is transcended.

We so pass into that 'divine darkness' of which Dionysius speaks, which appears dark only because it is pure light. We must ascend to that state of 'unknowing' in which all human knowledge fades away, and we shall know truly 'even as we are known.'

In this view of the ultimate mystery of being, which is the beginning and the end of all our human aspirations, Hindu, Buddhist and Christian unite and in God all differences which appear in nature, and all distinctions known to the human mind, are transcended.

Knowledge and love

God cannot be imagined or conceived. Knowledge of God emerges from a kind of unknowing, a passing beyond all images and concepts into the darkness of unknowing.

This is the knowing of the heart, not of the intellect. It is therefore the knowledge of love. This love itself flows from God, the source, for there is in God a pure act of self-giving by which he ceaselessly communicates himself.

This love is mirrored in the mystery of the Godhead. The Father knows himself in the Son and the Son in the Father. Father and Son communicate in the love of the Holy Spirit.

Unity in God

All our conflicts arise because we stop at a certain level. Christians stop at the Christin religion, Muslims at Islam, and if you are a Hindu you stop at your own symbolism. Each one feels himself separate from the others. Only when you go beyond these distinctions and are open to the reality beyond, can you overcome these conflicts.

The ultimate reality includes all the differences in the world. It does not abolish them. You and I are all contained in the Absolute.

We see everything separated, but if you have the vision of reality you perceive all the differences in that total unity.

We have to get beyond limited mental perceptions and even parapsychological perceptions to a pure spiritual wisdom, a vision where the whole universe is seen as a total unity in the Absolute Godhead, and we ourselves as one in this Absolute, each a unique manifestation of the one eternal reality.

Science and spirituality

Today we are on the threshold of a new age. This is true for the Western scientific disciplines, for psychology and also for spirituality.

Physics has discovered that matter is not the solid substance it was previously supposed to be. It is a field of energies and with that field of energies there is consciousness.

Psychologists are discovering that there is such a thing as transpersonal consciousness, where human beings can go beyond previously understood limits and there become open to a transcendental consciousness.

Here we find an opening up of Western thought to that of the East. The previously dismissed so-called psuedo-science of the East is now profoundly affecting Western thought and the boundaries between science, psychology and spirituality are disappearing.

Scientific motivation and centuries of belief in a mechanistic universe are giving way to the perceptions of an organic universe. This understanding has always existed at the level of Hindu, Buddhist and Taoist philosophy. All this is at the heart of the new age.

A Trinity of love

There is in the Godhead a pure will of love, a pure act of self-giving by which he ceaselessly communicates himself.

As the Father knows himself in the Son, and the Son in the Father, so Father and Son communicate in the love of the Holy Spirit.

The Holy Spirit is this expression of love within the Godhead, the relation of love which unites the persons of the Godhead. Yet there is no 'duality' but an identity of nature and consciousness in the bliss of love.

The bliss of the Godhead is the overflowing love of God, the mysterious communication of love within the Godhead.

The world of resurrection

It is an illusion to think that the Kingdom of God will come in this world or that lasting peace and joy will be established on earth.

This is the great 'maya' or illusion which deceives the world and which veils the truth.

This illusion arises from the refusal to face death. For those who seek fulfillment in this world death is an end, a boundary that cannot be passed. But for those who are willing to die, death is the gateway to eternal life.

The new world which we seek is the world of the resurrection. Yet this world is already present among us, for 'the kingdom of heaven is in your midst' (Luke 17:21). Death is the breakthrough to a new consciousness, a consciousness which is beyond the senses and beyond the mind and opens up the eternal and the infinite. We may only catch glimpses of it now, but it is speaking throughout the world. 'The former things have passed away...Behold, I make all things new' (Revelation 21:4, 5).

Prayer

To pray is to enter consciously into communion with God or the Source.

At its highest peak prayer becomes contemplation. Here it is wordless. It is a merging of human consciousness with the Divine.

At the center of the prayerful state is the stilling of the mind. 'Be still, and know that I am God,' says the psalmist (Psalm 46:10).

Prayerfulness opens up a channel between the soul and God, so there is intercommunion between the human and the Divine.

Prayer stems from meditation, for the latter is preparing the ground for the former.

Prayer may be conceived of as a descent into the depths of the heart and as a rising towards the Godhead. In the opened heart is the prayer that does not cease.

The cave of the heart

Today many aspects of Hinduism are becoming well known in the West. More and more young people are visiting India and discovering what they recognize as a 'mystical religion,' and which speaks to their longing to 'know God.' So there is an increasing desire in the West to understand the religion of the Hindus.

Where do we begin? To start with doctrines leads to endless debate. There are innumerable Hindu doctrines which one can compare with similar Christian doctrines, but it is only when one comes to the level of interior experience that a real unity takes place.

Father Le Saux, a French Benedictine monk, describes this sharing of a common experience in his book *Hindu-Christian Meeting Point in the Cave of the Heart:* 'We have to live the Hindu experience of God and learn to live it from the depths of our experience of God's revelation in Christ.' This is to meet in 'the cave of the heart.'

The cosmic dance

One of the great figures of Indian mythology is the dancing Shiva. He is represented with four arms, dancing in a circle of fire, dancing at the heart of creation. It is a cosmic dance; it represents the power which permeates the whole universe.

The idea is that God is dancing in the heart of creation and in every human heart.

If we find the Lord who is dancing in our hearts then we will see the Lord dancing in all creation. Shiva holds a drum in his upper right hand. This is the sign of creating the vibration of sound from which creation comes. The word *Om* is held to be the original sound. It is a reminder of the Greek Alpha and Omega, the beginning and the end which embraces all words, all meaning, all sound. In his upper left hand Shiva holds fire, the symbol of destruction. The whole world is continually being created and destroyed.

This is the rhythm of creation, the order of creation which is sustained by God.

Beyond thought

The rational mind always thinks in terms of duality; subject and object, mind and matter, body and soul, time and space. These are all categories of the rational mind.

These categories are of course valuable and necessary, for they enable us to operate within the world of time and space, the world of sense perception. We cannot discard them, but as we begin to contemplate so we go beyond these dualities. We transcend reason and logical thought, and open ourselves to the direct experience of the spirit. This is the unifying experience.

Thoughts may take us to the furthest outreach of space, but they neither find nor relate to God. God cannot be realized or known by the processes of the mind. Thought can give birth to further thoughts about God.

The hope of humanity today is to get beyond the experience of duality. A spiritual awakening in this direction is taking place all over the world. Beyond thought is where, in the words of St Paul, we find God to be 'all and in all' (1 Corinthians 15:28).

A sense of the sacred

Everything in India has a sacred character. It meets on every side—they are living in a sacred world. Here in the West we live in a profane world. For the last three centuries we have tried to reduce everything from the sphere of the sacred, the sphere of God.

Science tries to eliminate the sacred; the moon is not something sacred. It has become simply a chemical formation about which we seek to learn all we can. The same is true of the earth and the other planets. So we have eliminated two dimensions of reality, the psychological and the spiritual. We begin to think that the world is one-dimensional, that it is only material. We forget the sacred character of the whole creation. The incarnation of Christ is the great historical affirmation that all matter is sacred.

Christ and history

The suffering, death and resurrection of Christ have a universal meaning, a meaning for all and an effect upon history.

Through Christ's death and resurrection human history has been changed. Mankind has been changed because mankind is ultimately one, an organic interdependent whole extending through time and space.

Christ's death and resurrection extend to all humanity, both in the past and in the present and in the future. In that sense it is also a mythological event. It is symbolic yet also historical.

Here history has assumed a universal meaning. Creation and the whole of humanity find ultimate meaning and purpose in that death, resurrection, ascension and final glorification.

All this is to be found in St Paul's conception of the mystical Body of Christ which is the 'fullness of him who fills all in all' (1 Corinthians 15:28).

Humanity fulfilled

The world today is striving to attain a more complete humanity, to enable every man to realize his total personal being in a society which respects the human person. The human person is constituted by its experience both of physical reality in the world to which it belongs and of the social reality of the persons with whom it lives in communion. This whole world therefore of physical and social relationships is included in the sphere of contemplation. This is not to be found in separation from the body and society but in the transfiguration both of the body and of society, by which the total human being achieves its growth to full personal being, 'to mature manhood, to the measure of the stature of the fulness of Christ,' as St Paul describes it (Ephesians 4:13).

Perfect contemplation is attained therefore only through the struggle to achieve the total interpretation of the human personality in all its dimensions.

To find fulfillment man has to transcend himself, to discover a dimension of being beyond both the physical and the mental, and where the physical world itself is transfigured and is no more subject to corruption and death. This is the world of the resurrection, the 'new creation' of St Paul.